EXCEL FUNCTIONS AND FORMULAS

Shortcuts, Formulas and Functions for Business Modeling and Financial Analysis

Sarah Jones

TABLE OF CONTENT

Introduction

As a beginner, it is important for you to master the basic and advanced Excel formulas and functions as this would make you become very proficient in financial analysis and business modeling.

Financial analysis and business modeling apply in several parts of our lives whether work life or personal life. Most companies and individuals depend on Microsoft Excel in performing their analysis and modeling needs.

Microsoft Excel is seen as the ideal software for data analysis while the spreadsheet program is one of the most preferred software by financial analysts and bankers in processing data, financial modeling and presentation.

In this book, I would teach you all you need to know to become an expert in using Excel for your financial analysis and planning.

Part of what you would learn from this book include

- Important Excel shortcuts and why you should use shortcuts
- Excel terminologies explained
- The different data types you would encounter while using Excel
- Advanced Excel Formulas and functions
- Over 150 list of Excel functions you should know and how to use them
- Using Excel to Perform Valuation Modeling
- And lots more

My goal for writing this book is to ensure that you are able to confidently make use of Excel whether for personal or work needs. The book contains screenshots of examples to further explain each points and topic. This would serve as your guide in achieving greater success with Excel and spreadsheets.

Excel Shortcuts

Using shortcuts or shortcut keys while working with Excel would help to increase your productivity. With the shortcut keys you are able to perform major functions without having to click the toolbar and this would increase your speed. Imagine when you just have to press two or three keys on the keyboard instead of having to touch the mouse, move the move and clicking several times. Excel has several keyboard shortcuts that you can use to increase your productivity. These shortcuts can be used to perform several functions, from simple ones like moving within the spreadsheet to inputting formulas or grouping your data.

It may seem a little slow in the beginning since you are used to mouse, but its important you take out time to learn these important shortcuts.

The first task that would be required of you if you are hired as an investment banking analyst is to take some intense Excel training courses. During these courses, you would not be allowed to make use of your mouse and you would have to learn financial modeling using only the keyboard shortcuts. If you follow the tips and tricks I would talk about here, you would be a master of these shortcuts in no distant time.

Basic Excel Shortcuts Terminologies

Let us first familiarize ourselves with the basic terminology around the elements of Excel.

Cell: This is any of the several boxes seen on the Excel spreadsheet

Active cell: this is the current cell selected on the Excel worksheet. You can only have one active cell. In other words, the active cell is the cell you are using to input your formulas or data at the time.

Row: while columns are vertical, rows are horizontal cells, referenced in Excel by whole numbers in an increasing order from no 1 to N. The number that ends N would depend on the version of Excel you are using and your operating system.

Column: This is a group of vertical cells referenced by letters in an ascending order of A to Z. After it gets to column Z, Excel begins a repeat of the letters a second time. So, after Z, the next column is AA, AB etc.

Selection: this is either the active cell or a group of cells selected within the worksheet

List of Excel Shortcuts

The shortcuts listed below are specific for persons using Windows PC.

For Editing

F2 – to edit active cell

Ctrl + C – to copy

Ctrl + X – to cut

Ctrl + V – to paste

Alt+E+S – to paste special

Alt + Enter – begin a new line inside same cell

F3 – to paste name inside a formula

F4 – to toggle references

Shift + F2 – edit or insert cell comment

Shift + F10 – performs same function as right click; shows the shortcut menu

Shift + F11 – to insert a new worksheet

Ctrl + F3 – title a cell

Ctrl + D – to copy contents down from the previous cell (fill down)

Ctrl + R – fill right

Ctrl + Shift + A – inserts argument names and parentheses for a function after you have typed name of a function in a formula

Alt + I + R – insert new row

Alt + I + C – Insert column

For Formatting

Ctrl + 1 – Pops up the menu for format cells

Ctrl + B – To make data bold

Ctrl + I – for italics

Ctrl + Z – to undo

Ctrl + Y – redo

F4 – To repeat your last action

Ctrl + A – To select all the used cells/ selects the entire worksheet if you repeat the command

Ctrl + Shift + ! – to format number

Ctrl + Shift + # - to format date

Ctrl + Shift + % - to format percent

Alt + h + fg – to increase font size

Alt + h + fk – to reduce font size

Alt + h + o – for increasing decimal places

Alt + h + 9 – to reduce decimal

Alt + h + 6 – to increase dent

Alt + h + 5 – to reduce indent

For Navigation

Arrows – to move around the cells, left, right, up and down

F5 – for Go to

Ctrl + Home – to return to cell A1

Home button – to go to the beginning of a row

Shift + Arrow – selects the adjacent cell

Shift + Spacebar – to highlight the whole row

Ctrl + Spacebar - to highlight the whole column

Ctrl + Shift + Home – selects all from the active cell to the start of the sheet

Ctrl + Shift + End – selects all to the last cell used in the worksheet

Ctrl + Shift + Arrow - selects all to the last cell used in the column or row

Ctrl + Arrow - Move to the last used cell in the column or row

Pageup - Moves one screen up

PageDown - Moves one screen down

Alt + PageUp - Move one screen to the left

Alt + PageDown - Move one screen to the right

Ctrl + PageUp/ Down - Move between tabs if in a menu window or move to the previous or next worksheet

Ctrl + Tab - move to the next divider while in menu options and move to the next workbook under the spreadsheet

Tab - go to the next cell

Clear Shortcuts

Alt + h + e + m – to clear all cell comments

Alt + h + e + f – to clear cell formats

Alt + h + e + a – to clear every including formats, data and comments

Delete – clear data from the cell

File Shortcuts

Ctrl + N – open new workbook

Ctrl + O – To open

Ctrl + S – to save your workbook

F12 – to Save As

Ctrl + P – to print

Ctrl + F2 – display the print preview window

Ctrl + Tab – Move to the next workbook

Ctrl + F4 – to close file

Alt + F4 – to close all excel files that are open

Paste Special

Ctrl + Alt + V + v – to paste special values

Ctrl + Alt + V + T – to paste special formats

Ctrl + Alt + V + c – to paste special comments

Ctrl + Alt + V + f – to paste special formulas

Ribbon Shortcuts

Ctrl + F1 – Hide/ show ribbon

Alt – to show the ribbon accelerator keys

Selection Shortcuts

Shift + Arrows – to select a range of cells

Shift + PageDown – to extend the screen selection one screen down

Shift + PageUp – to extend the screen selection one screen up

Ctrl + Shift + Arrows – Highlight from the active cell to the last filled cell on the movement

Ctrl + A – Selects the whole workbook

Alt + Shift + PageUp – to extend selection from active cell to one screen to the left

Alt + Shift + PageDown - to extend selection from active cell to one screen to the right

Data Editing Shortcuts

Ctrl + R – Copies right to the active cell what exist on the left cell

Ctrl + D – Copies down to the active cell what exist on the above cell

Ctrl + F – find and replace

F5 + Alt + s+ c - Highlights all cells with comments

F5 + Alt + s+ c – Display all constants

Editing Data Inside Cell

F2 – to edit the active cell

Enter – Accepts change and exit the cell

Esc – To cancel entry in a cell and exit the cell

Alt + Enter – To type another paragraph or line break in a cell

Shift + Right/ Left – To highlight contents within a cell

Ctrl + Shift + Right/ Left – to select all contents inside a cell from where the arrow is placed

Home – return to the beginning of the cell contents

End – Move to the end of the active cell

Backspace – delete data backwards

Delete – erase data from the front

Tab – accept the suggestions from autocomplete

Ctrl + PageDown/Up + Arrows – Reference a cell from a different worksheet

Other Shortcuts

Ctrl + Shift + : - To enter the current time

Ctrl + ; - To enter today's date

Ctrl +] – select cells that refer to the active cell

Ctrl + ` - Show values / formulas

Alt – Brings up the menu bar

Alt + = - to autosum

Alt + Tab – press down to display all open programs on the laptop, click on tab until you get to the next program you want to access

Examples of Excel shortcuts

	A	B	C	D
1		Price	Quantity	Total Price
2	Orange	$ 1.00	5	$ 5.00
3	Tomato	$ 2.00	10	$ 20.00
4	Potato	$ 3.00	20	$ 60.00

These pieces of data have only columns A to D and rows 1 to 4.

In this screenshot, the user has a selection of cells A2 to D2. This would show in Excel formula as A2:D2.

No matter how large a selection is, you can only have one active cell. In this screenshot, the active cell is cell A2 that has Orange as the text data.

Cells A2:A4 contains text data (Orange, Tomato and Potato)

Cells B1:D2 has the text data (Price, Quantity, and Total Price)

Cells B2:B4 and D2:D4 has the currency data represented by $

Cells C2:C4 has the number data

Basic Excel Terms

There are two ways you can perform calculations in Excel: Functions and Formulas.

1. Functions

Functions are formulas that have been predefined in Excel. With this, you won't need to do tasking manual inputting of formulas and they have names that are familiar with humans. For instance: =SUM (A1:A4). This would sum all the values in the boxes of A1 to A4.

2. Formulas

A formula in excel is an expression that works with values in a range of cells or in a cell. Example: =A2+A3+A4. This would give you the sum of the figures in the cell A2 to cell A4.

Types of Data Presented in Excel

Data presented in Excel are of different types. They include:

Text: these are data written as alphabets/ letters. You can also have numbers in the text data, but they have to be used together with letters or you manually set them to text.

Numbers: these are data that are written as numbers strictly. Unlike text data where you can have numbers combined with text, you cannot combine letters with the number type data.

Percentage: this data type is a subset of numbered data that are turned into percentage. You can convert them back to number type data and vice versa. If you convert a percentage data type to a number type, the number will be shown as a decimal. For example, 79% will show as 0.79.

Currency/ accounting: these pieces of data makes use of numbers and a currency marker

Dates: this type of data represent time and/ or date. Excel gives option of multiple formats to write the date.

Ways to Input Data in Excel

When performing data analysis, there are 5 main ways you can input basic Excel formulas. Whichever method you decide to go with all has their own advantages. Before we go into the main formulas, I would explain these methods so that you can pick choose your preferred workflow now.

1. Simple insertion: type the formula inside the cell

Typing the formula straight in the cell or in the formula bar is the most direct way you can insert the basic Excel formulas. You begin by using the equal sign (=) followed by the name of the function (e.g. SUM)

Excel has been built in a way that once you begin to type the name of the function, a popup hint would appear. You can select your preferred function from the list. After you have selected your desired function, do not use the Enter key but press the Tab key so that you can continue to type in other options. If you click on the Enter key, Excel would most likely return an invalid name error usually displayed as '#NAME?'. To correct this, double click on the cell to open it for editing and then you complete the function or you click on the cell and go to the formula bar at the top of the excel page to complete the function.

2. **Select a Formula from one of the Groups in the Formula Tab**

If you want to quickly delve into your favorite functions, this method is for you. To locate this menu, go to the formulas tab and choose your preferred group. Click on it and you would see a sub menu filled with a list of different functions. From there, you can choose the one you want to use. However, if your preferred group is not in the tab, click on the "More Functions" option, you may just see it hidden there.

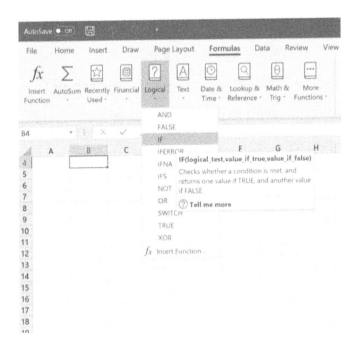

3. Using Insert function option from formula tab

If you want to have total control of your functions input, using the Excel insert function dialogue box is what you need. To do this, go to the formulas bar and click on the first menu labeled as 'Insert Function.' Once the dialogue box opens, you would see all the functions you need to perform your financial analysis.

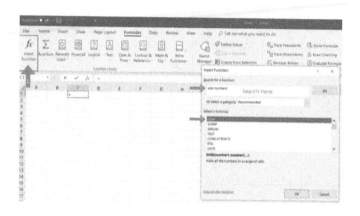

4. Quick Insert: Make use of Tabs used recently

If you do not like retyping the formulas that you used recently, you can make use of the Recently Used menu. You would find this on the Formulas tab, it is the third menu option after the AutoSum.

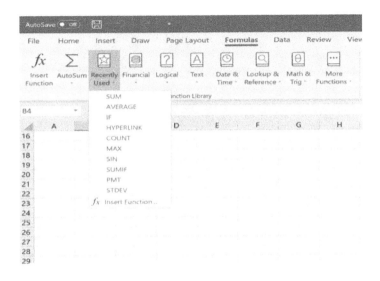

5. Using the AutoSum option

If you need to perform a task quickly, you should use the AutoSum functions. To get to this function, go to the Home tab, then click on the AutoSum option at the right corner of the screen. Then click on the caret to display other hidden formulas. You would also see this option in the Formulas tab. It is the first option you would come across after you click on the Insert Function option.

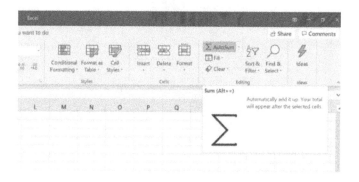

Basic Excel Formulas for your Workflow

Now that you are able to insert your preferred function and formulas correctly, let's look at some fundamental Excel functions.

1. Average

This is same as the simple averages of data or numbers like the average number of employees in a given employee pool

The formula for this is =AVERAGE (number1, [number2], ...)

Examples

=AVERAGE (B2:B11) – this is similar to the formula (SUM (B2:B11)/10), it adds all the numbers in the range and gives an average of it.

	A	B	C
1	**Country**	**Population**	
2	China	1,389,618,778	
3	India	1,311,559,204	
4	USA	331,883,986	
5	Indonesia	264,935,824	
6	Pakistan	210,797,836	
7	Brazil	210,301,591	
8	Nigeria	208,679,114	
9	Bangladesh	161,062,905	
10	Russia	141,944,641	
11	Mexico	127,318,112	
12	**Average**	=AVERAGE(B2:B11)	Output = 4,358,101,991
13			
14			

2. SUM

This function should be the first Excel formula you should know. It adds the values in selected rows or columns within your selected range.

=SUM (number1, number 2....)

For example:

=SUM (B2:G2) – this selection would sum the values in the row B2 to G2.

=SUM (A2:A8) – this selection would sum the values of a column, in this case, column A2 to A8

=SUM (A2:A7, A9, A12:A15) – this is a sophisticated collection that sums values in a range of column. In this example, the Excel would sum the values in A2 to A7, skip A8 and add A9, jump A10 and 11 and then adds from A12 to A15.

=SUM (A2:A8)/20 – with this, you can also convert the functions into formula.

File   Home   Insert   Draw   Page Layout   Formulas   Data   Review   View   He

Paste	X Cut 🗋 Copy · 💅 Format Painter		Calibri B *I* U ·	· 11 · · 🖎 · 🔺 ·	A˙ A˙	≡ ≡ ≡ ≡	≡ ≡	⚓ · ⫶⫶
	Clipboard	Ɡ		Font				Alig

SUM   ·   ✕   ✓   *fx*   =SUM(B2:B11)

◢	A	B	C
1	**Country**	**Population**	
2	China	1,389,618,778	
3	India	1,311,559,204	
4	USA	331,883,986	
5	Indonesia	264,935,824	
6	Pakistan	210,797,836	
7	Brazil	210,301,591	
8	Nigeria	208,679,114	
9	Bangladesh	161,062,905	
10	Russia	141,944,641	
11	Mexico	127,318,112	
12	**Total**	=SUM(B2:B11)	Output = 4,358,101,991
13			
14			

3. COUNT

This Count function counts all the cells in a selected range that has only numbers in them.

Formula for this is =COUNT (Value1, [value2],...)

For example

COUNT (A:A) – counts all the numerical values contained in B column

You can however adjust the range inputted in the formula to also count the rows.

COUNT (A1:C1) – Now this formula has also put in rows in consideration.

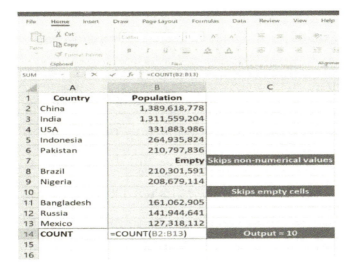

4. COUNTA

This is similar to the COUNT function as this counts all the cells in any range that you select. The only difference is that this one counts all the cells whether numbers or not. While COUNT chooses just numbers, the COUNTA counts times, dates, errors, logical values, strings, text or empty string.

=COUNTA (value1, [value2],...)

Examples

COUNTA (C2:C13) – this would count from rows 2 to 13 in column C whether they are numbers or not. Remember that this formula did not consider columns, only rows. You can double click on the cell to add the option for column inside the brackets. An example of this is **COUNTA** (C2:H2) to count columns C to H

AutoSave ● Off 🖫

File   Home   Insert   Draw   Page Layout   Formulas   Data   Review   View   Help

✂ Cut   Calibri   · 11 · A A   ☰ ☰ ☰ ❖ ·
📋 Copy ·
Paste
  ✎ Format Painter   B I U · ▭ · ◇ · A ·   ☰ ☰ ☰ ☷ ☷

      Clipboard   ⌐   Font   ⌐   Alignmen

SUM   ·   ⌐   ✕ ✓ fx   =COUNTA(B2:B13)

◢	A	B	C
1	Country	Population	
2	China	1,389,618,778	
3	India	1,311,559,204	
4	USA	331,883,986	
5	Indonesia	264,935,824	
6	Pakistan	210,797,836	
7		Empty	Counts all values
8	Brazil	210,301,591	
9	Nigeria	208,679,114	
10			ONLY Skips empty cells
11	Bangladesh	161,062,905	
12	Russia	141,944,641	
13	Mexico	127,318,112	
14	COUNTA	=COUNTA(B2:B13)	Output = 11
15			

5. TRIM

This function eliminates any errors that may occur as a result of unruly spaces. It removes all the empty spaces. TRIM can only operate on a single cell unlike the other functions that can work with a range of cells. The downside of this is that you may end up having repeated data in your spreadsheet

=TRIM (text)

Example

TRIM(A2) – removes all empty spaces in the value of cell A2.

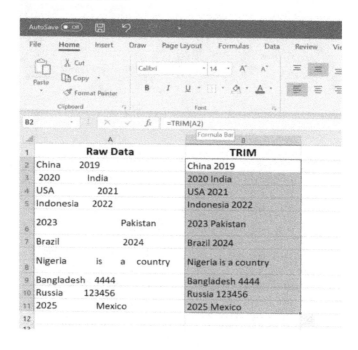

6. IF

You use this when you want your data to follow a specified logic. This means that you give Excel some conditions in which it would use to sort the output of the data. The best part of this formula is that you can include functions and formulas in it.

=IF (logical_test, [value_if_true], [value_if_false])

Examples

=IF (C2>D3, 'TRUE,' 'FALSE') - this is used to check if the value of D3 is lesser than the value of C3. If the logic is true, the cell value would be TRUE, if not, cell value would be FALSE.

=IF (SUM (C1:C10) > SUM (D1:D10), SUM (C1:C10), SUM (D1:D10)) – this is a complex example of the IF logic. First, it adds up C1 to

C10 then D1 to D10 before comparing the sum of C and D. If the sum of the C1 to 10 is higher than the sum of D1 to 10, it then becomes the value of a cell = the sum of C1 to 10. If not, it becomes the SUM of C1 to 10.

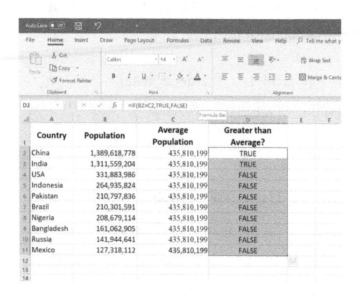

7. MAX AND MIN

This function helps you to find the minimum and maximum number in a pull of values.

=MIN (number1, [number2],...)

Example:

MIN (B2:C11) – would find the minimum number between Colum B, beginning from B2 and column C, starting from C2 to roll 11 for column B and C together.

MAX (number1, [number2],....)

Example:

=MAX (B2:C11) – in same way, it finds out the maximum number between column B starting from B2 and column C from C2 to row 11 in the two columns.

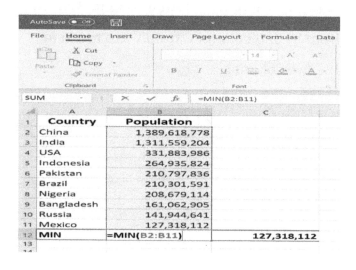

Advanced Excel Formulas

As a financial analyst, you tend to use Excel more than you like. Based on tears of experience, this part if the book would talk about the most important and the advanced Excel formula that is a must know for every world class financial analyst.

1. **CELL, LEFT, MID and RIGHT functions**

When you combine these functions, it would give you some advanced and complex formulas. The CELL function can give variety of information about contents of a particular cell like the name, row, column, location and lots more. The LEFT function can return text starting from the beginning of a cell (left to right), MID returns text located at any point of the cell (left to right), and the RIGHT functions returns text starting from the end of the cell (right to left).

You would see an example of these 3 formulas being used below:

	A	B	C	D	E	F
1						
2						
3		New York, NY		=LEFT(B3,3)	⇨	New
4						
5				=MID(B3,5,4)	⇨	York
6						
7				=RIGHT(B3,2)	⇨	NY
8						
9						
10						
11						

2. INDEX MATCH

Formula for this is =INDEX (C3:E9, MATCH (B13, C3:C9,0), MATCH (B14, C3:E3,0))

This formula is an advancement on the HLOOKUP or VLOOKUP formulas (these ones have their own limitations and

44

drawbacks). **INDEX MATCH** is a powerful tool that combined different Excel formulas to take your financial modeling and analysis to the next level.

INDEX converts the values in a cell into a table using the row and column number.

MATCH returns the cell position in a column or row.

Below I have given an example of a combination of INDEX and MATCH formulas. For this example, we find and return a person's height using their name. Because the height and the name are variables in the formulas, we can change them both.

	A	B	C	D	E	F	G
1							
2			1	2	3		
3		1	Name	Height	Weight		
4		2	Sally	6.2	185		
5		3	Tom	5.9	170		
6		4	Kevin	5.8	175		
7		5	Amanda	5.5	145		
8		6	Carl	6.1	210		
9		7	Ned	6.0	180		
10							
11							
12			=INDEX(C3:E9,MATCH(B13,C3:C9,0),MATCH(B14,C3:E3,0))				
13		Kevin					
14		Height					

3. OFFSET combined with AVERAGE or SUM

The Formula for this is =SUM (B4: OFFSET (B4,0, E2-1))

The offset function is not exactly advanced, it becomes advanced when you use together with other functions like AVERAGE or SUM. Assume you need a dynamic function that can add up the variable number of cells. Using just the SUM formula, you would be limited to a static calculation but when you add the OFFSET formula, you would have a cell reference that can move around.

For this formula to work, we replace the ending reference cell of the SUM function with the OFFSET function.

This would help make the formula to be dynamic and with the cell titled E2, you can let Excel know how many consecutive cells you want to add together. Now this is an advanced formula.

I have included a screenshot to explain this formula

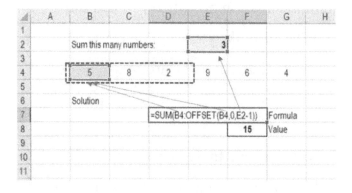

As seen in the screenshot, the SUM formula begins in cell B4 but has a variable at the end which is the OFFSET formula that started from B4 and continued to the value in E2 ("3"), minus one. This would take the end of the SUM formula over 2 cells, summing the data for 3 years plus the starting point. As seen in cell F7, adding up cells B4:D4 would give you 15, which is same as what we got with the offset and SUM formula.

4. Combination of IF with OR/ AND

The formula is =IF(AND(C2>=C4, C2<=C5), C6, C7)

If you have spent some time doing different types of financial models, you would agree with me that nested IF formula can be a terror. To keep your formulas easier for others to understand and for audit reasons, you can combine IF with the AND or the OR function. The example below shows how I combined the individual functions to give a more advanced formula.

	A	B	C	D	E	F	G
1							
2		Data Cell	150				
3							
4		Condition 1	100	>=			
5		Condition 2	999	<=			
6		Result if true	100				
7		Result if fales	0				
8							
9		Live Formula	=IF(AND(C2>=C4,C2<=C5),C6,C7)				
10							
11							

5. CHOOSE

The formula for this is =CHOOSE (choice, option1, option2, option3)

This is great when you have to analyze a scenario in financial modeling. With this formula, you are able to pick between specified number of options and give back the "choice" that you selected. For instance, say you have 3 different revenue growth assumptions for next year, 5%, 12% and 18%. With this formula, you can return the 12% if you input #2 as your choice.

	A	B	C	D	E	F	G
1							
2							
3			Option 1	5%			
4			Option 2	12%			
5			Option 3	18%			
6							
7		Selection ->	2	=CHOOSE(C7,D3,D4,D5)			
8							
9							
10							
11							

6. XIRR and XNPV

Formula: =XNPV (discount rate, cash flows, dates)

If you are working as an analyst in equity research, investment banking or financial planning and analysis, or other areas of corporate finance that needs discounting cash flows, this formula can be a lifesaver.

This is to say that this the XIRR and XNPV allows you to use exact dates to each individual cash flow that you want discounted. The problem with the basic formula NPV and IRR is that they use equal time periods for all the cash flows. As you work as an analyst, you would come across situations where the cash flows are not equal in dates and periods, in such cases, you can fix using this formula.

	A	B	C	D	E	F	G	H	I
1									
2									
3		Dates		5/18/2018	12/31/2018	9/12/2019	12/25/2019	5/8/2020	12/31/2020
4									
5		Cash Flows		1,000	1,000	1,000	1,000	1,000	1,000
6									
7		Discount Rate		10.0%					
8									
9		XNPV	=XNPV(D7,D5:I5,D3:I3)		Formula				
10				5,289	Value				
11									

7. SUMIF and COUNTIF

The formula for this is =COUNTIF
(D5:D12,">=21")

These two formulas are great to use for
conditional functions. SUMIF adds all the
cells that meet preset conditions and the
COUNTIF counts all the cells that meets the
pre-set conditions. For instance, say you want
to count all the cells that have figures greater
than or equal to 21, using the legal drinking
age in the U.S, to give you an idea of how
many bottles of champagne you should get for

a client's event, you can do this using
COUNTIF as I would show you in the
screenshot below:

◢	A	B	C	D	E	F	G	H
1								
2								
3								
4				Age				
5				19				
6				26				
7				20				
8				19				
9				29				
10				31				
11				21				
12				25				
13								
14				=COUNTIF(D5:D12,">=21")				
15								

8. LEN and TRIM

Formulas: =LEN (text) and =TRIM (text)

Although these are not common, but they are
still quite sophisticated. These formulas are
great if you work as a financial analyst and

need to organize and manipulate a large volume of data. Unfortunately, the data we get are not always organized perfectly and at other times you can have issues like extra spaces at the end or the beginning of the cells.

I have used the example below to show you how you can clean up the Excel data with the TRIM formula.

	A	B	C	D	E	F	G
1							
2							
3		No Extra spaces					
4		Exampl of extra spaces			=TRIM(B4)		
5							
6					⬇		
7		Example of extra spaces			Example of extra spaces		
8							
9							
10							

9. PMT and IPMT

Formula: =PMT (interest rate, # of periods, present value)

If you work in real estate, commercial banking, financial planning and analysis or any other financial analyst role that deals with debt schedules, then you need to understand these two detailed formulas.

With the PMT formula, you are able to get the value of equal payments over the loan life. You can also use it together with IPMT (this gives you the interest payment for that loan) then separate the interest payments from the principal.

In the screenshot below, I have shown an example of how you can use the PMT function to give you the monthly mortgage payment for a $1 million mortgage with interest rate of 5% for 30 years tenure.

	A	B	C	D	E
1					
2					
3		Rate	5.0%		
4		# Periods	30		
5		Loan Value	1,000,000		
6					
7		PMT	=-PMT(C3,C4,C5,,1)	Formula	
8		PMT	61,954	Value	
9		Monthly PMT	5,163		
10					

10. CONCATENATE

Formula: =A1&" more text"

We cannot really call this a function on its own, rather let's say this is an innovative way of adding information from several cells and makes the worksheets more dynamic. This tool is powerful for handling financial modeling.

The example below shows you how the text "New York" plus ", "is joined with "NY" to give us "New York, NY". This would enable you to create dynamic headers and labels in worksheets. Now, instead of directly updating cell B8, you can independently update cells B2 and cell D2. This skill is usually valuable when dealing with large set of data.

◢	A	B	C	D	E	F
1						
2		New York		NY		
3						
4						
5		=B2&", "&D2				
6		⬇				
7						
8		New York, NY				
9						
10						
11						

List of Excel Functions

Below I have added a list of over 150 Excel functions to help you achieve faster results with financial analysis. Remember to use an equal sign (=) before typing in any of the formulas below. Excel has been built in such a way that once you begin with an equal sign and then type the function, a drop down would pop on your screen, guiding you on what parameters you should include. I have explained when to use each of these functions.

For Financial

CUMIPMT

This would give you the cumulative interest paid on a loan

CUMPRINC

You use this to get the cumulative principal paid on a loan.

ACCRINT

Use this function to calculate accrued interest for a security whose interest is paid periodically

ACCRINTM

This is used to get the accrued interest for a security that issues its interest upon maturity.

DOLLARDE

Convert dollar value from decimal place to fraction

DISC

Calculate the rate of discount applied on a bond.

DB

To calculate the depreciation of an asset.

DURATION

Use this for the duration of a security

INTRATE

This gives you the interest rate for a security

IPMT

Get the principal for any specified period.

EFFECT

Get the yearly interest rate as well as the number of compounding interest for each year.

MDURATION

Use the Modified Macauley Method to get the duration of a security

FV

This stands for Future value, for calculating the future value of an investment.

FVSCHEDULE

Calculate the future value of an investment by using a variable interest rate.

IRR

Calculate the Internal Rate of Return for a specified cash flow

ISPMT

Used to know the interest paid at a specified period of any investment

MIRR

Gives you the modified internal rate of return for a specified period of a cash flow.

NOMINAL

For getting the nominal annual interest rate

NPV

Gives you the Net Present Value for a periodic cash flow

NPER

Get the number of periods for an investment or a loan

PDURATION

This helps you know how long, that is, fixed number of periods or time it would take an investment to reach a certain value

PRICE

Get the price of a bond for every $100 face value

PRICEDISC

Get the price of a bond for every $100 face value of a security that is discounted

PRICEMAT

Calculate the price of a bond that gives interest at maturity for every 100$ face value.

PMT

Gives you the expected payment per period for a loan.

PPMT

Calculate the payment on the principal of a loan or an investment

PV

This gives you the current value of an investment

RATE

Gives you the interest rate for each period of an annuity

RECEIVED

Gives you the amount gotten at maturity of a security that was fully invested

SLN

Shows the depreciation of an asset on a straight line

SYD

Gives you an asset's "sum-of-years' depreciation

VDB

This uses the Double Declining method to get the depreciation of an asset

TBILLPRICE

Get a treasury bill's fair market value

TBILLEQ

This would convert treasury bill yield to a bond equivalent

TBILLYIELD

Gives the return on a treasury bill

XIRR

Gives the internal Rate of Returns for several cash flows that are not periodic

YIELD

Gives the return on a security

YIELDDISC

Get the annual return for a security that is discounted

YIELDMAT

Gives the yearly return on a security

NXPV

Gives the Net Present Value for some series of cash flows that are usually not periodic.

For Date and Time

DAY

This function shows the day as a number from 1 to 31 using a date

DAYS

Get the days between two or more dates shown as a number 1 to 31

DAYS360

If you need to get the days between two dates in a 360 days year then use this function

Date

This is to quickly get today's date and it would appear as year, month and day.

DATEDIF

Use this to find years, months or days between two dates

DATEVALUE

Change a date shown in text format to the valid date

EDATE

This would duplicate the same date in past or future date.

EOMONTH

This function gives the last day of the month for past or future months

MINUTE

Get the minute of an inputted time written as a number 0 to 59

HOUR

Input a time in a cell and use this function to give you the hours of that number in number 0 to 23.

MONTH

Input a date in the cell and get the month of that date written as number 1 to 12.

ISOWEEKJUM

This function would give you the ISO week number from any date you input.

NETWORKDAYS

Get the number of working days between two dates you input.

NETWORKDAYS.INTL

Get the works days spelt out between two dates you input.

NOW

This function gives the exact time and date as at when you are performing the function.

SECOND

Get the second from a time written as a number 0 to 59.

TODAY

Get today's date

TIME

Create the time written in hours, minutes and second.

TIMEVALUE

Used to get the real time from a string of text.

WEEKDAY

This gives the day of the week written as a number.

WEEKNUM

Get the number for the week in a given date.

WORKDAY

Get the dates of work days in the past or future.

WORKDAY.INTL

This gives date and working days in the past or future.

YEAR

This function picks out the year from given dates

YEARFRAC

This function gives you the fraction of a year between two dates

Logical

IF

Test to see that a certain condition is met

IFERROR

This trap and handles error

IFNA

Gives a specified alternate value whenever a formula returns an N/A error

IFS

Use to test several conditions, return first true

AND

Checks out multiple conditions using AND

OR

Test several conditions using OR

XOR

Perform an exclusive OR

FALSE

Create Logical value, FALSE

NOT

Reverse results or arguments

SWITCH

Tests a given expression and gives back a result to correspond to the first matching value.

TRUE

Make the logical value TRUE

ENGINEERING

CONVERT

Converts the unit of measurement

INFO

Gives information about a current location or environment

CELL

Shows information about a cell

ISERR

Test for all other errors minus #N/A

ISERROR

Use this to check for every possible error

ERROR.TYPE

Test to check a specific error value

ISBLANK

This would show you if there are any blank cells

ISEVEN

Shows whether a value is even or not

ISLOGICAL

Used to check that a value is logical

ISFORMULA

Use this to see if a cell has formulas in it

ISNONTEXT

Check for a value that is not text

ISNUMBER

Check for number values

ISNA

Check for the N/A error

ISODD

Use this to confirm whether a value is odd or not

ISREF

Check for a reference

ISTEXT

Checks for a text value

NA

Generate an A/N error

N

Convert to a number from any value

TYPE

Shows the type of value you have in a cell

Math

ARABIC

Convert a numeral from Roman to Arabic

ABS

Gives the absolute value of a number

BASE

Turn a number into the supplied base

CEILING

This rounds up a number to the closest specified multiples

CEILING.MATH

Round up a number to the closest integer or multiple of significance

COMBIN

For getting the total number of combinations

COMBINA

Gives the total number of combinations with repetitions included

EVEN

Rounds up a number to the next integer that is even

DEGREES

Turn radians to degrees

ISO.CEILING

Have a number rounded up to the closest multiple of significance or nearest integer.

MOD

Gives the remainder from a division

MROUND

Round up a number to the nearest multiple specified

PI

Gives the value of pie

ODD

This rounds up a number to the next odd number

RAND

Gives a random number between 0 to 1

RANDBETWEEN

Gives a random whole number between two values

ROUND

This rounds a number up to the number of digits you desire.

ROUNDDOWN

Rounds down a number to your desired number of digits

ROUNDUP

Rounds up a number to your desired number of digits

Lookup and Reference

AREAS

Gives the numbers of areas in a reference

HLOOKUP

Find a value in a table by matching on the first row.

ADDRESS

Use a given column and row to create a cell address

CHOOSE

Pick a value from a list of positions

FORMULATEXT

Shows the formula contained in a cell

COLUMN

Gives a reference's column number

COLUMNS

Gives the number of columns in a reference or array

GETPIVOTDATA

Retrieve data from a pivot table in a formula.

HYPERLINK

Create a link that you can click on

INDIRECT

Form a reference from text

INDEX

Find a value in a table or a list using location

LOOK UP

Find a value in a one column range

MATCH

Find an item's position in an array

OFFSET

Generate a reference offset from a specified starting point

TRANSPOSE

Flip the orientation of a group of cells

RTD

Import real time data from a COM automation server

ROW

Find the row number of a reference

ROWS

Find the number of roles in a reference or array

VLOOKUP

Find a value in a table using a method of matching on the first column

Valuation Modeling in Excel

This refers to the several different types of analysis which includes comparable trading multiples, discounted cash flow (DCF), ratios such as horizontal and vertical analysis and then precedent transactions. You can build the analysis mentioned here from scratch with excel or you may want to use an already done template or model. This type of work is usually done by finance professionals.

Performing Valuation Modeling in Excel

There are several reasons why you should use Excel for valuation modeling and different professionals in various industries spend quality time doing this type of work.

The reasons include

- Legal proceedings like insolvency

- Preparation to raise capital from investors (and deciding what price shares should be issued at)
- Impairment testing (this is similar to any significant re-education in the values of assets)
- Evaluate capital projects and investment opportunities
- Knowing how much to pay for a business you wish to acquire
- A business succession planning
- For issuing shares to employees
- For planning and internal budgeting purposes
- Selling a business and knowing how much to accept for the sales

Ways to Perform Valuation Modeling in Excel

As we have already stated above, we have 3 main methods of evaluating a company. The most detailed of it is the Discounted cash flow or the DCF and is sometimes the most reliable approach. Below I have explained how to perform each of these modeling types.

Discounted Cash flow modeling

For this approach, a finance professional or an analyst would need to get 3 to 5 years historical financial information about a business and input on Excel. They then link the three financial statements together to get them dynamically connected. Once this is gotten, they now make assumptions about the future performance of the business. With these assumptions in Excel formulas, they now create a forecast for the future (usually about 5 years from the time the modeling is done). Lastly, they calculate the business's terminal value and then discount this forecast period and the terminal value back to the present using the company's weighted average cost of capital (WACC).

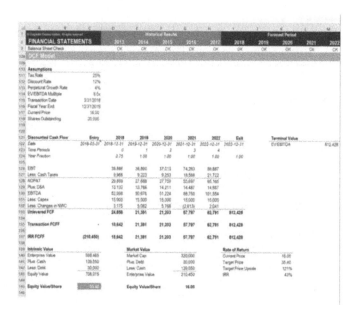

Comparable trading multiples in Excel

This method is different from the DCF model. In this Excel method, rather than getting a company's intrinsic value as is dome in the first step above, an analyst would look at the valuations of other companies that are publicly traded and compare these companies to the businesses they desire to value.

Popular examples of the valuation multiples are Price/Earnings, EV/EBIT, EV/EBITDA, ET/Revenue and Price/Book.

Company Name	Market Data					Financial Data (FY+1)			Valuation (FY+1)		
	Price ($/share)	Shares (M)	Market Cap ($M)	Net Debt	EV ($M)	Sales ($M)	EBITDA ($M)	Earnings ($M)	EV/Sales x	EV/EBITDA x	P/E x
Micro Partners	$9.45	100	$945	$125	$1,070	$268	$76	$47	4.0x	14.1x	20.1x
Junior Enterprises	$5.68	1,250	$7,100	$2,000	$9,100	$4,136	$778	$412	2.2x	11.7x	17.2x
Miniature Company	$18.11	50	$906	$25	$931	$443	$96	$56	2.1x	9.7x	16.3x
Average Limited	$12.27	630	$7,730	$350	$8,080	$1,949	$528	$294	4.1x	15.3x	26.3x
Behemoth Industries	$9.03	1,500	$13,545	$0	$13,545	$6,622	$796	$423	2.0x	17.0x	32.0x
Average									2.9x	13.6x	22.4x
Median									2.2x	14.1x	20.1x

Precedent transaction modeling

In this 3rd approach, the analyst would look at the prices paid for mergers and acquisitions (M and A) of companies in similar businesses done in the past. This form of valuation is quite relative but unlike the comparable trading multiples, these transactions include takeover premiums; this is the value of control, and the comparisons are based in the past which can become outdated quickly.

Date	Target	Transaction Value ($M)	Buyers	Sales	EBITDA	EBIT	EV/Sales	EV/EBITDA	EV/EBIT
01-24-2018	Current Ltd	2,350	Average Limited	1,237			1.9x	na	na
04-19-2016	Recent Inc	6,500	Bohemeth Industries	4,643	808	515	1.4x	8.0x	12.6x
04-19-2014	Past Co	2,150	Other Group	1,693	249	178	1.3x	8.7x	12.1x
11-07-2014	Historical LLP	450	Junior Enterprises	197			2.3x	na	na
11-01-2012	Old Group	325	Minature Company	64	17	15	5.1x	18.8x	21.5x
10-07-2011	Dated Enterprises	150	Micro Partners	71	16		2.1x	9.3x	na
Average							2.3x	11.2x	15.4x
Median							2.0x	9.0x	12.6x

Skills Needed to Perform Valuation Modeling in Excel

To perform this type of analysis as a finance professional, you would need to get several skills that may take some years of experience and education to master.

The most important of these skills are

- Finance (formulas, financial math, calculations and ratios)
- Accounting (financial statements, methods, principles)
- Strategy (market analysis and competitive advantage)
- Excel (shortcuts, MS Excel best practices, functions)
- Valuation (this includes a combination of all the skills above)

Jobs that Require Valuation Modeling

Before you can get some jobs or seek career path in these jobs, you should be skilled in valuing a company, an investment opportunity or a business unit in Excel

Some of these popular jobs are

- Corporate development (as an analyst or manager)
- Equity research (for associate and analyst level)
- Venture capital and private equity (as an analyst and associate)
- Public accounting (impairment testing, transaction advisory)
- Financial planning and analysis (analyst, manager and director level)
- Investment banking (as an analyst and an associate)

Reasons to Use Excel for Valuation Modeling

While Excel can be a blessing, it can also be a curse. At times bigger organizations attempt to use other software for their financial modeling but end up returning to Excel.

The main reasons for this are

- Cost of purchase is quite low
- Very simple to use and can be easily audited
- Ubiquitous and well understood for several people
- Easy to customize and totally flexible
- You can easily share with third party

On the other hand, the flexibility that comes with using Excel means that the models can be prone to errors, poor practices and inaccurate calculations. Finance professionals and analysts have to ensure that they possess a good excel modeling skills and a sharp understanding of best practices in the leading industry.